D R Y

DRY

DELICIOUS HANDCRAFTED COCKTAILS
AND OTHER CLEVER CONCOCTIONS

SEASONAL. REFRESHING.
ALCOHOL-FREE.

CLARE LIARDET

THE EXPERIMENT
NEW YORK

DRY: *Delicious Handcrafted Cocktails and Other Clever Concoctions—Seasonal. Refreshing. Alcohol-Free.*
Copyright © 2017, 2018 by Transworld Publishers

Originally published in Great Britain by Bantam Press, an imprint of Transworld Publishers, in 2017.
First published in North America by The Experiment, LLC, in 2018.

The Experiment, LLC | 220 East 23rd Street, Suite 600 | New York, NY 10010-4658
theexperimentpublishing.com

Many of the designations used by manufacturers and sellers to distinguish their products are claimed as trademarks. Where those designations appear in this book and The Experiment was aware of a trademark claim, the designations have been capitalized.

The Experiment's books are available at special discounts when purchased in bulk for premiums and sales promotions as well as for fund-raising or educational use. For details, contact us at info@theexperimentpublishing.com.

Library of Congress Cataloging-in-Publication Data

Names: Liardet, Clare, author.
Title: Dry : delicious handcrafted cocktails and other clever concoctions :
    seasonal, refreshing, alcohol-free / Clare Liardet.
Description: New York, NY : The Experiment, LLC, 2018. | Includes index. |
    Identifiers: LCCN 2018014464 (print) | LCCN 2018022662 (ebook) | ISBN
    9781615195060 (Ebook) | ISBN 9781615195022 (cloth)
Subjects: LCSH: Cocktails. | Non-alcoholic beverages. | LCGFT: Cookbooks.
Classification: LCC TX951 (ebook) | LCC TX951 .L53 2018 (print) | DDC
    641.87/4--dc23
LC record available at https://lccn.loc.gov/2018014464

ISBN 978-1-61519-502-2
Ebook ISBN 978-1-61519-506-0

Cover and text design by Sarah Smith
Cover photograph by Jason Ingram
Author photograph © 2017, 2018 by Clare Liardet
Photographs by Jason Ingram
Illustrations by Beci Kelly

Manufactured in China
First printing October 2018

10 9 8 7 6 5 4 3 2 1

CONTENTS

INTRODUCTION

Whether you're the designated driver, a teetotaler, pregnant, having a go at Dry January, trying to lose weight, or just cutting down, most of us will want a break from alcohol at some point. And an alcohol-free period is a brilliant opportunity to go wild with adventurous and delicious drinks.

More ingredients than ever before are available to experiment with: There are alcohol-free brewers around every corner, nonalcoholic spirits, and even new varieties of many classics like tonic water. A few of the recipes in this book need a little forethought and some do include the odd unfamiliar ingredient, but most can whipped up with what you're likely to have at hand in the kitchen or garden.

Dry has plenty of inspiring examples of imaginative, grown-up, nonalcoholic alternatives, and there's definitely something for everyone. So whether you're planning a Friday night in with friends, a lazy Sunday brunch, or a barbecue in the summer sun, you can find your dry drinks here.

EQUIPMENT

THE BASICS

Shaker

If you choose to invest in one piece of equipment, this is where I'd recommend you spend your money. I prefer a two-piece, all-metal shaker, as not only is it handy for packing into a basket for outings, it chills the drink quickly and with less dilution than ice. However, if you don't own one, a large jam jar will do!

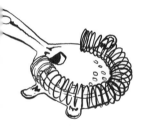

Strainer

Many of these recipes require a strainer and a Hawthorne-style strainer is particularly useful. Make sure it's well made and that it's not loose where the handle meets the circle of the strainer. Alternatively, you could use a small fine-mesh sieve or a slotted spoon.

Muddler

This is a long pestle for crushing the oils out of zest or leaves, and mixing in sugar. They come in a variety of materials but wood is preferable as it does a gentler job than metal—even the end of a small rolling pin or wooden spoon would do.

Bar spoon

This is a fun piece of equipment to have but certainly not essential. It's a very long-handled teaspoon, but a chopstick will do.

Squeezer

Fresh juice always makes such a difference in a dry drink, so I'd highly recommend investing in a squeezer. I love a hinged, stainless-steel press. They're easy to use with limes, lemons, and oranges, and release the citrus oils, too.

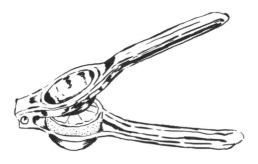

Knife, cutting board and peeler

You'll use a small, sharp knife and a handy cutting board all the time with these recipes. Just make sure that your knife is super sharp. I prefer using a Y-peeler, as it can also make lovely wide ribbons of whatever you need.

Measure or jigger

At home you don't need a strict bar measure, but it's useful to have on hand something that's consistent. I use a small glass measuring cup that has both fluid ounces and milliliters marked on the side. Tablespoon and teaspoon measures are handy to have, too.

Juicer

If you're going to be experimenting with and exploring juices, a centrifugal juicer is a perfectly adequate and not-too-expensive piece of equipment. From experience, I'd recommend finding one that's easy to take apart to clean.

Blender

A blender of some sort is really useful—it could be a canister, NutriBullet, or hand-held stick. I recently splurged on a really powerful one and haven't looked back. It can whip up a frozen drink, crush ice or coffee beans, and make nut milk with ease, plus it's also fabulous for soup making.

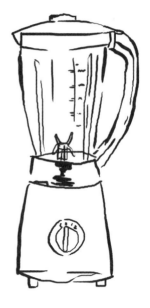

SodaStream

If you like making sparkling drinks, this machine can save you a lot of time and money in the long run. The end result doesn't necessarily replace a good-quality sparkling mineral water, but it can add instant fizz to any drink.

Glass pitcher for mixing or serving

A medium-size thick glass pitcher that can hold the right amount of ice is all you need. A handle will ensure the drink stays as cool as possible.

Canning jars, jam jars, and bottles

These are great for storing sugar syrups or shrubs. You'll need to sterilize them before use and there are two main ways of doing this:

1. The Oven Method. Preheat the oven to 285°F (140°C) / 250°F (120°C) convection. Wash the jars in hot, soapy water, and then rinse them well. Place the jars on a baking sheet and put them in the oven to dry completely. This will take about 15 minutes. If you're using canning jars, sterilize the rubber seals separately, in a pan of boiling water for a few minutes, as dry heat from the oven will damage them.

2. The Dishwasher Method. Fill your dishwasher with clean jars and run it on the hottest setting, or a steam setting if it has one. Once the cycle has finished, leave the jars to cool in the dishwasher.

GLASSES

The world is your oyster here, and I encourage you to have fun. You can spend a small fortune on traditional and beautiful glassware, but a French jam jar or a quirky, mismatched selection of glasses from a flea market can be just as fabulous. Heat-resistant glasses are fun, as unlike traditional mugs they allow the color of the drink to show. I have a selection of different-sized inexpensive Duralex ones.

In a traditional cocktail, the shape of a glass has a role to play in the way the drink is served. A few classic shapes are listed below.

1. **Highball** – narrow and thin, this holds fizz well
2. **Sling** – elegant, tapering at the bottom
3. **Tumbler** – short and heavy-bottomed
4. **Martini or cocktail** – small and delicate V-shaped cup on a stem
5. **Flute** – narrow and elegant on a stem, this holds fizz well
6. **Champagne coupe, sour, or daisy** – larger open cup on a stem

① ② ③

④ ⑤ ⑥

INGREDIENTS

On the pages that follow is a collection of staples that I try to have in my kitchen at all times. None of them are difficult to find—you should be able to pick them up from a supermarket or buy them online.

FRUIT AND VEGETABLES

I'd urge you to use organic fruit and vegetables whenever possible, and if you're using the peel of citrus fruits try to find unwaxed varieties as wax will inhibit the release of oils. I think it's essential to have plenty of lemons and limes in the kitchen, and it's important to make sure you taste any seasonal fruits before you start preparing your drinks, as their sweetness can vary.

BITTERS

Bitters typically contain around 47% alcohol by volume, but you will only ever use a few drops at a time. They add complexity and depth to the flavor of a drink and, although it can be a little time-consuming to do so, it's very easy to make your own.

CELERY SALT

Simply made by mixing equal quantities of salt and ground celery seeds, it's easy to whip up fresh celery salt at home.

FRESH GINGER

A fiery rhizome or root that has antibacterial, anti-inflammatory and antiviral properties.

JASMINE TEA FLOWERS

Green tea leaves are wrapped around a jasmine flower to form a ball that when steeped in hot water, unfurls to reveal the flower within. They can be used to make a delicately flavored and lightly scented tea.

KOMBUCHA

An ancient fermented tea made using a SCOBY (Symbiotic Culture of Bacteria and Yeast). It's full of probiotic cultures and, once brewed, is said to be great for the immune and digestive systems. There are many different flavors available in shops.

HIMALAYAN SALT

Mined in the Punjab region of Pakistan, this salt has a wonderful rose color and is said to contain many minerals and trace minerals.

RAW HONEY

Raw honey hasn't been heated to high temperatures and so retains its beneficial nutrients. It's been used by different cultures for hundreds of years for its medicinal properties. Try to buy local, untreated honey if possible.

ROSE WATER

Not to be confused with the more concentrated rose essence, rose water is made by steeping rose petals in water, and has been used for centuries as a flavoring.

TAMARIND

This bean-like fruit pod from the tamarind tree contains pulp and many seeds. It's used extensively in Southeast Asian cooking and tastes a little like a tart, lemony date. Interestingly, it is a key ingredient in Worcestershire sauce.

TURMERIC

This rhizome looks like a slimmer version of ginger but is a bright yellow-orange and can help clear infections and reduce inflammation in the body. Try to find fresh turmeric, but if you can't, the powder is great, too.

SMALL BOTTLES OF GOOD-QUALITY MIXERS

A selection of ginger ale, ginger beer, and tonic is essential. Some personal favorites are listed at the end of this section on page 25.

I've also included just a couple of lesser-known ingredients in these recipes. They might not be in your supermarket, but they can be found online or in health food shops.

MONTMORENCY CHERRY CONCENTRATE

A nutritious, tart cherry juice rich in phenolic acids.

SICHUAN (OR SZECHUAN) PEPPERCORNS

These originate from the Sichuan province of China and are not actually pepper, but the dried berries of a type of ash tree. They have a warm, spicy, citrusy aroma.

Don't Forget

Herbs and spices have been used for medicinal purposes for centuries, so if you're pregnant or on medication it's worth checking which, if any, you should avoid. *Jekka's Complete Herb Book* is my garden bible, but do check with your doctor. Also be careful with grapefruit juice, which affects the way your body metabolizes certain medications.

GARNISHES

Citrus

Make lengths of peel using a Y-peeler and twist them over the rim of the glass to release the essential oils that will then float on the surface of the drink. Alternatively, you can use wedges or wheel-shaped slices.

Herbs

Use fresh herbs and try to avoid tearing or bruising the leaves. Whack them gently on a hard surface to release their aroma and flavor before putting them in a glass.

Edible flowers

My favorites are roses, violets, elderflowers, white and blue borage, and lavender. Unsprayed organic flowers are best.

Scented geranium leaves have been used for hundreds of years to add wonderful flavor but, like the bay leaf, aren't pleasant to actually eat.

ICE

You'll need lots of ice, so make sure you have space in the freezer. The more ice you put in a shaker, the quicker the drink will chill and the more it will dilute. Equally, the larger the ice cube, the less dilution there will be.

Shapes

Be imaginative! Use silicone molds or a plastic tub if you need a large block of ice for a pitcher. Alternatively, snipping the dividers out of a silicone ice cube tray (carefully, with a pair of scissors) will give you long blocks. To make crushed ice, put some cubes in a clean cloth, tie the four corners together and smash against a solid surface.

Flavors

Think about freezing leftover juices, watermelon slices, or halved lemons. These can be very useful when cooling a large pitcher, as too much melting ice will dilute the flavor of the drink.

Flowers and leaves

Freezing a flower or a few leaves in an ice cube can make a great visual addition to a drink. I particularly like using blue borage flowers or celery leaves for savory tipples.

Flavored Waters

It's so simple and easy to have a pitcher of chilled, flavored water on a table. I like to add:

- Cucumber, apple, and tarragon
- Peach, raspberry, pomegranate, and mint
- Strawberry and melon
- Mixed citrus fruits with mint

If you're organized, you can make a large pitcher the day before you need it and leave it to infuse overnight. Just add ice and extra water before serving.

A Note on Sugar

We all know that processed white sugar is best avoided, and thankfully there are some great alternatives available these days. While clear sugar syrup requires white sugar (and this is definitely worth doing for special occasions!), you can also use superfine sugar. The syrup will look slightly colored, but will still taste great.

Here are a few other alternatives:

Stevia A natural sweetener, about 300 times sweeter than sugar, from the *Stevia rebaudiana* plant. To me it has a faintly chocolaty taste.

Brown rice syrup Made from fermented cooked rice and complex carbohydrates.

Maple syrup A unique taste that is great added to Hot Buttered Spiced Apple (page 111) if your apples are a bit tart.

SYRUPS AND SHRUBS

Sugar syrups are easy to make and will happily keep in the fridge for a week or two. I tend to make small batches and store them in sterilized and labeled jam jars or bottles. They give an unusual depth and layer of flavor to drinks, particularly those that are alcohol-free. Shrubs are an alternative to fruit cordials and are also easy to make at home. The word *shrub* originates from the Arabic *sharbah*, which means "drink."

Simple Herb or Flower Syrup

The intensity of an herb's flavor varies throughout the year, so you might need to experiment with these lovely syrups. Just use a teaspoon to test the strength as it simmers, and adjust as necessary.

Makes a 13.5-ounce (400 ml) bottle

1 cup (200 g) sugar
¾ cup (200 ml) water
Herb/flower of choice, for example:
a few good sprigs of mint
2 to 3 tablespoons lavender buds
12 lemon verbena leaves
2 sprigs of rosemary
a sprig of rose-scented geranium leaves
a dried hibiscus flower

Put the sugar and water in a pan on a low heat, stirring constantly, until the sugar dissolves. Bring the syrup to a simmer, add your chosen herb or flower and then continue to simmer for 5 to 10 minutes more. Remove from the heat and allow to cool. Strain the syrup into a sterilized bottle.

Rhubarb Syrup

Makes a 24-ounce (700 ml) bottle

10 stalks (500 g) rhubarb, trimmed of leaves and roughly chopped
¾ cup (200 ml) water
1¾ cup (350 g) sugar

Put the rhubarb in a pan with the water. Bring to the boil and then simmer until the rhubarb has almost completely broken down. This should take around 30 minutes.

Strain the cooked rhubarb through a clean piece of cheesecloth (this will take a few hours), collecting the liquid in a bowl beneath.

Add the strained liquid to a clean pan with the sugar and bring to a simmer. Once the sugar has dissolved, leave to cool before transferring to a sterilized bottle.

When you're happy making the basic syrup, you can experiment a little. Perhaps add 4 strips of orange peel to the rhubarb in the pan, or 8 to 10 whole star anise for a spicier edge. If you want a sharper flavor, add the juice of 3 lemons when you add the sugar.

Smoky Lapsang Syrup

Makes a 17-ounce (500 ml) bottle

1 cup (250 ml) water
2 Lapsang Souchong tea bags
1¼ cup (250 g) sugar

In a pan, bring the water to a boil and add the tea bags. Take off the heat and leave to steep for 15 minutes. Once cool, remove the tea bags and add the sugar. Stir gently over a low heat until the sugar has dissolved, then bring to a simmer. Leave to cool again before transferring to a sterilized bottle. This is an intense-flavored syrup, so take care how much you add to your drinks!

Ginger and Black Peppercorn Syrup

Makes a 27-ounce (800 ml) bottle

9 ounces (250 g) fresh, unpeeled ginger, chopped into small pieces
1 tablespoon coarsely crushed peppercorns
1 quart (1 L) water
2 cups (400 g) sugar
Pinch of sea salt

Place the ginger, peppercorns, water, sugar, and salt in a pan. Bring to a boil, then reduce the heat to a steady simmer for 45

minutes. Allow to cool, then strain the syrup through a fine-mesh sieve into a sterilized bottle.

Black Currant or Berry Shrub

Makes a 10-ounce (300 ml) bottle

2 heaping tablespoons raw honey
½ cup (125 ml) organic apple cider vinegar
4½ cups (500 g) black currants or a 16-ounce (500 g) bag of frozen berries of your choice

In a pan, warm the honey with the vinegar so that the honey melts but doesn't boil. Place the fruit in a mixing bowl and add the honeyed vinegar so that it just covers the fruit. Crush to mix using the end of a rolling pin, then transfer the mixture to a sterilized 17-ounce (500 ml) jar. Put the lid on the jar and shake well. Leave somewhere cool for 3 to 4 days (or longer if you put it in the fridge), and shake once a day. Strain through a jelly bag or clean cheesecloth placed over a bowl, allowing the juice to drip through overnight. Then, using a funnel, decant the juice into a sterilized bottle. It can be stored in the fridge for a month and used like a cordial.

Chile-Infused Syrup

Makes a 13.5-ounce (400 ml) bottle

¾ cup (200 ml) water
1 cup (200 g) sugar
4 red chiles, sliced in half lengthwise

Add all the ingredients to a pan and bring to a boil. Allow them to bubble for 5 minutes until thickened slightly. Remove from the heat and set aside to cool. Pour into a sterilized jar or bottle.

Spice Syrup

Makes a 25-ounce (750 ml) bottle

1 cup (250 ml) water
½ cinnamon stick
1 teaspoon black peppercorns
2 green cardamom pods
Pinch of grated nutmeg
10 coriander seeds
1 star anise
2-inch (5 cm) piece of fresh ginger, chopped
2½ cups (500 g) sugar
Strip of orange peel

Put the water in a pan and bring to a boil. Bash the spices in a mortar with a pestle and add them to the boiling water with the ginger, sugar, and orange peel. Stir and remove from heat. The longer you leave the spices to infuse, the more intense the syrup will be. I would recommend a minimum of 1 hour. Allow to cool, then strain through a fine-mesh sieve into a sterilized bottle.

Hibiscus Syrup

Makes a 20-ounce (600 ml) bottle

2 cups (500 ml) water
Scant ½ cup (90 g) white sugar
Scant ¼ cup (35 g) light brown sugar
⅓ cup (15 g) dried hibiscus flowers
Zest of 1 lemon

Add all the ingredients to a pan and bring to a boil. Reduce the heat and allow to simmer until the sugars dissolve and the flowers soften. This should take about 10 minutes. Remove from the heat and steep the syrup for around 5 minutes until the flavors combine. Strain the syrup into a sterilized bottle through a fine-mesh sieve. Press any solid ingredients with the back of a spoon to extract as much liquid as possible before discarding.

MY FAVORITE QUICK FIXES

There's a growing market of interesting, grown-up, blessedly nonsweet, alcohol-free drinks out there. Here are a few that I think are definitely worth having in the cupboard, ready to grab at the drop of a hat. The last three may be hard to find in stores, but are available from online retailers.

Seedlip Marketed as the world's first nonalcoholic distilled spirit, Seedlip is doing something unique. There's a range of flavors and you'll find Garden #108—a fresh and summery flavor—and Spice #94—which is more wintery—used in recipes in this book. They're delicious with tonic or when added to a cocktail, and they offer a depth and complexity that belies their lack of alcohol.

Fever-Tree Tonics Delicious either on their own or when used as a mixer. Experiment with different flavors and combinations. I particularly love their elderflower tonic water.

Teetotal G 'n' T Currently only sold in the UK, these flavored tonics from the Temperance Spirit Company are perfect with ice and a slice.

Crodino This is a delicious, bitter aperitif from the company behind Aperol and Campari.

San Pellegrino Sanbitter There are two different versions: Dry, which is clear, and Red, which looks like Campari.

Double Dutch Produced by Dutch twins Joyce and Raissa, these mixers are divine and I'd highly recommend the summery Cucumber & Watermelon flavor.

NEW STARTS

These are drinks with bright, clean flavors, perfect for new beginnings and setting new goals. Whether it's the start of the year or a moment for pausing and reflecting, there are options here to set you on your way, to get you out of the door, or to welcome you home.

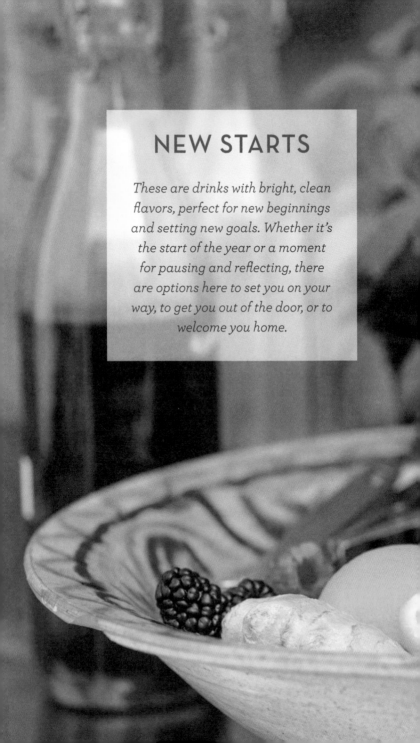

Blood Orange Sunrise

Serves 2

You will need

2 tumblers

Ice cubes

3½ ounces (100 ml) fresh pomegranate juice

Juice of 1½ blood oranges

Juice of ½ lime

1½ teaspoons honey

Plain or sparkling water

2 twists of blood orange peel and a few pomegranate seeds to garnish

1 Place a handful of ice cubes in each tumbler and divide the pomegranate juice between the 2 tumblers.

2 In a small bowl, whisk together the blood orange juice, lime juice, and honey.

3 Divide the mixture from the bowl between the glasses and top with a splash of plain or sparkling water, a twist of blood orange peel, and a few pomegranate seeds.

. . . .

FLAVOR Blood oranges have a short season (from late winter to early spring) but their rich ruby juice is a must-try. Slightly tarter than that of a normal orange, it's full of anthocyanins, a family of antioxidant pigments common to many flowers and fruit, but uncommon in citrus fruits. With a hit of pomegranate juice, this is a great kick-start to your day.

ADAPT To make a longer drink for later in the day, add 1⅔ cups (400 ml) ginger ale or ginger beer.

Nimbopani

Serves 2

You will need
blender; 2 tumblers

Juice of 6 small
South Asian lemons
or 3 large lemons

4 to 5 tablespoons
superfine sugar

1½ teaspoons sea salt

Sprig of mint or 6 mint
leaves, plus more to
garnish

Ice cubes

❶ Blend the lemon juice, sugar, and salt together until frothy.

❷ Add the mint leaves and blend for 5 seconds more.

❸ Serve over ice in a glass and garnish with mint leaves.

INSPIRATION For me, this drink tastes of India. I can almost smell the heat and hear the honking horns. On a very warm day when you're feeling dehydrated, there's nothing more refreshing than this intense little number. It's a fantastic pick-me-up after exercise, too.

ADAPT For an equally delicious alternative, use six juicy limes instead of lemons.

Tropical Morning Smoothie

Serves 2

You will need
*blender; 2 large
stemmed glasses*

½ large ripe pineapple,
  peeled, cored, and cut
  into chunks

½ large ripe papaya,
  peeled, seeded, and cut
  into chunks

1 teaspoon vanilla extract

¾ cup (200 ml) full-fat
  coconut milk

Juice of 1 lime

½ teaspoon ground
  turmeric

⅔ cup (150 ml) coconut
  water or water

Small piece of fresh
  ginger, peeled
  (optional)

Ice cubes

❶ Blend the pineapple, papaya flesh,
vanilla extract, coconut milk, lime juice,
turmeric, coconut water, and ginger (if
using) together until smooth and frothy.
Add more water if necessary.

❷ Pour over ice and enjoy right away, or
transfer to a thermos to keep cool for later.

....

HEALTHY Refreshing, anti-inflammatory,
and full of antioxidants, this is a great
smoothie to wake up to. Alternatively, it
makes the perfect post-workout treat.

Raw Spicy Mary

Serves 1

You will need

juicer; highball

3 ripe plum tomatoes

1 celery stick, trimmed

½ red bell pepper, seeded

½ red chile, seeded

1 teaspoon organic apple cider vinegar

Juice of ½ small lemon

1 teaspoon extra virgin olive oil

Large pinch of sea salt

1 wedge of lemon to rim the glass

Himalayan salt, or another pinch of sea salt

Ice cubes

Freshly grated horseradish or freshly ground black pepper to garnish

Celery stick to stir

1 Wash the tomatoes, 1 celery stick, bell pepper, and chile, then push them through the juicer.

2 Stir in the cider vinegar, lemon juice, olive oil, and the large pinch of salt. Taste and adjust the flavors, if necessary. There should be a lovely balance of sweet, salty, and spicy.

3 Stir well before pouring into a glass rimmed with lemon juice and Himalayan salt, and filled with ice cubes. Finish with a sprinkling of fresh horseradish or black pepper, and a celery stick to stir.

. . . .

FLAVOR This is a really fresh and aromatic take on a Virgin Mary. It's a feast for all the senses, from the heady scent of ripe tomatoes to the vibrant color and sweet-hot tingle on the tongue. A true wake-up call.

Pineapple Mint Green

Serves 2

You will need
blender; 2 highballs

1 heaping cup (40 g) organic spinach

1 cup (40 g) chopped lettuce

¼ large ripe pineapple, peeled, cored, and cut into chunks

1 ripe pear, peeled and cored

½ banana (if the pineapple isn't ripe enough)

1 teaspoon flaxseeds

10 mint leaves

Juice of ½ lime

Ice cubes

❶ Wash the spinach and lettuce, and add them with the pineapple and pear to the blender. Check for sweetness and add the banana, if necessary.

❷ Add the flaxseeds and mint leaves, and blend thoroughly until smooth, then add lime juice to taste.

❸ Stir well and pour on top of the ice or into a thermos for a post-workout boost.

....

HEALTHY This is a lovely, fresh, fragrant green juice that's easy to make at the beginning of the day. It uses pear rather than apple, so isn't too sugary, and pineapple is a rich source of minerals, enzymes, and vitamins. This is a powerhouse start to the day.

Fiery Ginger and Apple Boost

Serves 1

You will need

juicer; tumbler

2 small sweet apples, cored

½ cup (50 g) peeled and sliced fresh ginger

Ice cubes

3½ ounces (100 ml) sparkling water

1 teaspoon agave syrup (optional)

Slice of apple to garnish

❶ Chop the apples to fit the juicer, then add in the ginger and blend.

❷ Pour 5 ounces (150 ml) of the apple-and-ginger mix into a glass of ice, and top with sparkling water. Stir in a little agave syrup to taste, if the apples are too tart. Garnish with a slice of apple.

FLAVOR I love the taste of ginger in the morning and have a guilty love of ginger beer at any time of the day. This is an instant, healthy, fizzy ginger hit, with none of the vast amounts of sugar found in commercial brands of ginger beer. It's completely invigorating.

Ginger, Turmeric, and Chile Tea

Serves 2

You will need

teapot; trainer (optional); 2 heatproof glasses or mugs

1 tablespoon finely grated peeled fresh ginger

½ teaspoon ground turmeric

Tiny pinch of cayenne pepper or a slice of red chile

¼ teaspoon black pepper (to aid turmeric absorption)

2½ cups (600 ml) very hot water

Juice of ½ lemon

A little raw honey

Slices of fresh ginger and lemon to garnish

1 Add the ginger to a teapot with the turmeric, cayenne, and black pepper.

2 Fill with very hot (but not boiling) water, stir, and then leave to steep for 10 minutes.

3 If you like, strain the liquid before pouring into heatproof glasses or mugs, then stir in the lemon juice and honey. Garnish with a fresh slice of ginger and lemon.

. . . .

HEALTHY This golden tea is a fabulous way to banish the winter blues and sniffles. The healing, immunity-boosting, and anti-inflammatory properties of ginger and turmeric have been used for centuries. This is a bit of warm sunshine on a chilly gray day.

Kiwi and Cucumber Juice

Serves 1

You will need
blender; highball

¼ large cucumber,
   roughly chopped

1 kiwi, peeled

½ pear, peeled and cored

Handful of watercress

½ celery stick, trimmed
   and roughly chopped

Leaves from 2 sprigs of
   mint

1½ teaspoons ground
   flaxseed

3½ ounces (100 ml)
   coconut water

Ice cubes

Slice of peeled kiwi to
   garnish

❶ Blend the cucumber, kiwi, pear, watercress, celery, mint, flaxseed, and coconut water until smooth, adding water if needed.

❷ Pour into a tall glass on top of a couple of ice cubes. Garnish with a slice of peeled kiwi.

....

FLAVOR A refreshing green juice for the morning, with plenty of goodness and fiber. Watercress is a true superstar in the world of nutrition, and I love this peppery hit to start the day.

FRIDAY NIGHTS

After a busy week, I often need a pick-me-up to start the weekend. And whether it's an impromptu gathering or a carefully planned party, I like to have some delicious ingredients in the fridge, ready to create a little something for myself or a recipe that can be scaled up to serve a group.

Blood Orange and Sage Margarita

Serves 1

You will need

shaker; strainer; chilled coupe

4 ounces (125 ml) blood orange juice

1 ounce (30 ml) freshly squeezed lime juice

½ ounce (15 ml) Hibiscus Syrup (page 24)

3 sage leaves

Ice cubes

Wedge of lime and himalayan salt (optional)

1 Put the blood orange juice, lime juice, hibiscus syrup, and 2 of the sage leaves in a shaker with ice, and shake until chilled.

2 If you like a salt rim, run a wedge of lime around the rim of the chilled glass and dip it in a saucer spread with salt.

3 Strain the mixture into the glass and garnish with the third sage leaf.

FLAVOR There is never a wrong time for a margarita in my book. The wonderful tart, salty tang of the drink is captured here and given depth with the hibiscus syrup. The sage provides an aromatic back note.

HEALTHY Blood oranges give the most beautiful juice, as well as being packed with antioxidants, so grab them in late winter or early spring when they're in season.

Blueberry Julep

Serves 1

You will need

muddler; tumbler or copper mug

¼ cup (40 g) blueberries

6 mint leaves

½ lime, cut into wedges

1 teaspoon sugar

Crushed ice

7 ounces (200 ml) ginger beer

Sprig of mint and a wedge of lime to garnish

❶ In a large glass, muddle the blueberries, mint leaves, lime, and sugar.

❷ Transfer to a tumbler or mug and add crushed ice, before pouring in the ginger beer and garnishing with the sprig of mint and wedge of lime.

FLAVOR This may be a simple recipe but it ticks all the boxes. The refreshing lime cuts through the warmth of the ginger, while the blueberries give the drink a tart sweetness. Juleps were traditionally served in pewter or silver cups, and held by the base or the rim, which helped to keep the drink cold.

Kombucha Spritz

Serves 1

You will need

pitcher; muddler; strainer; highball

1 inch (2 cm) rhubarb, sliced thin

3 strips of orange peel

2 teaspoons Montmorency cherry concentrate

4 ounces (120 ml) freshly squeezed orange juice

½ ounce (15 ml) Simple Herb Syrup made with rosemary (page 22)

Ice cubes

Wedge of lime

5 ounces (150 ml) kombucha

Dash of Angostura bitters (optional)

Twist of orange peel

Trimmed rhubarb stick to stir

❶ Place the sliced rhubarb in a pitcher with the orange peel and the cherry concentrate, and muddle to release the juice from the rhubarb. Add the orange juice and rosemary syrup, and muddle again.

❷ Strain into a highball full of ice, then squeeze in a wedge of lime and top up with the kombucha. If you wish to use Angostura bitters, add a dash now.

❸ Finish with a twist of orange peel dropped into the drink, and a stick of rhubarb to stir.

....

INSPIRATION Aperol Spritz makes me think of that delicious moment when the ski boots are off and everyone is gathered again, pink-cheeked, to talk about their day. I love the bitter notes in cocktails and was fascinated to read that Aperol lists rhubarb among its many ingredients. I think this many-layered drink belongs in the same family.

FLAVOR You may already be familiar with kombucha, a fermented tea made by combining bacteria, yeast, and sugar. It has a tart, sweet flavor, and you can either make your own or buy it ready-made.

Ginger, Lime, and Angostura Fizz

Serves 1

You will need

tumbler

1 ounce (30 ml) Ginger
   and Black Peppercorn
   Syrup (page 23)

Juice of ½ lime

Ice cubes

Sparkling water

A few dashes of
   Angostura bitters

Slices or wedges of lime
   to garnish

① Pour the ginger syrup into a tumbler
and add the lime juice.

② Half-fill the glass with ice and top
up with sparkling water. Shake in a few
dashes of Angostura bitters, stir, and add
the slices or wedges of lime to garnish.

FLAVOR This is a classic. It's simple
and delicious, yet often overlooked.
You can use bottled ginger beer instead
of the syrup (although you may need
more sparkling water to counteract the
sweetness), but in my eyes the heat of the
cordial makes it extra special.

Raspberry and Lavender Shrub

Serves 1

You will need
muddler; highball

2 sprigs of mint or
  lavender

1 ounce (25 ml) Berry
  Shrub made with
  raspberries (page 23)

Ice cubes

Juice of ½ lime

1 teaspoon Simple Flower
  Syrup made with
  lavender (page 22)

Sparkling water

Wedge of lime to garnish

❶ Lightly bruise the mint or lavender
sprigs with a muddler, then leave them in
the raspberry shrub for half an hour.

❷ Half-fill a tall glass with ice. Remove
the sprigs from the shrub and pour the
shrub over the ice.

❸ Add the lime juice to the glass, pour
in the lavender syrup and top up with
sparkling water. Garnish with a wedge
of lime.

....

INSPIRATION I love that shrubs have
a long history, dating as far back as
the Babylonians, and feel like elegant,
beautiful drinks. Here, lavender adds a
woody, floral element while the raspberry
shrub has an intensity and depth of flavor
that is missing in a simple cordial.

Peach and Lemongrass Cup

Serves 2

You will need

muddler; small pitcher; tumbler

½ stalk lemongrass, cut in half lengthwise

Large sprig of mint

1 ripe peach, sliced into wedges

1 cup (250 ml) unfiltered apple juice

1 lemon, thinly sliced

Ice cubes

Sparkling water

A stalk of lemongrass to stir

1 Muddle the lemongrass and the sprig of mint in a pitcher.

2 Add the peach, apple juice, and lemon, and leave to stand for at least an hour. This will help the flavors to develop.

3 Half-fill a tumbler with ice, pour in half of the juice, and top up with sparkling water. Add a lemongrass stalk to use as a swizzle stick.

....

FLAVOR This is a showstopper. It smells wonderful, and the woody, citrus notes of lemongrass stop it from becoming too sweet. This is one to make when the shops and markets are full of peaches and you can come home with a whole boxful.

Totally Citrus Fizz

Serves 1

You will need
muddler; tumbler

½ **stalk lemongrass,
outer leaves removed
and core roughly
chopped**

Ice cubes

1 ounce (30 ml) freshly
squeezed lime juice

½ ounce (15 ml) sugar
syrup

Sparkling water

Lemongrass stalk to stir

❶ Place the lemongrass in a tumbler and
muddle to release its oils.

❷ Fill the glass with ice and pour in the
lime juice and sugar syrup.

❸ Top up with sparkling water, stir
briefly, and garnish with the remaining
lemongrass stalk.

. . . .

INSPIRATION This is a drink to revive
and restore. The aromatic lemongrass
always sends me back to Brazil where, as
happens in the tropics, night falls quickly.
There's no time for languishing, and this
tipple brings the senses back to life, ready
for a Friday night.

Seedlip Asparagus Tonic

Serves 1

You will need

Y-peeler; tumbler; muddler

1 stalk asparagus

Ice cubes

1 ounce (25 ml) freshly squeezed lime juice

2 teaspoons (10 ml) Simple Herb Syrup made with rosemary (see page 22)

1½ ounces (50 ml) Seedlip Garden 108

Tonic water

Wedge of lime

Asparagus spear to garnish

❶ Using a Y-peeler, shear the stalk of asparagus lengthwise until you have a few shavings. Place these in the tumbler and press gently with a muddler.

❷ Half-fill the tumbler with ice and pour in the lime juice, rosemary syrup, and Seedlip Garden. Stir gently to mix, then top up with tonic water. Squeeze the wedge of lime over the top and garnish with the asparagus spear.

. . . .

INSPIRATION Right when the day is softening into evening, I love sitting in the garden for a moment. It's the perfect time to sip something delicious before cooking supper. This drink is green, fresh, and aromatic—just the thing to lift the fatigue of a long week.

LAZY SUNDAYS

Sunday brunch heralds a slower pace, a pause in the hectic modern week. It should feed all the senses, from the crisp opening of a newspaper to the aroma of freshly brewed coffee. Lazy limbs are roused slowly and taste buds can be awakened with an array of flavors.

Bloody Bull

Serves 1

You will need
shaker; highball

4 ounces (125 ml) tomato juice

4 ounces (125 ml) beef bouillon or homemade beef stock

½ teaspoon freshly grated horseradish

2 dashes of Worcestershire sauce

3 dashes of Tabasco sauce

Pinch of freshly ground pepper

½ ounce (15 ml) freshly squeezed lemon juice

Pinch of celery salt

Ice cubes

Wedges of lemon and lime to garnish

Celery stick to stir

❶ Add the tomato juice, beef bouillon, horseradish, Worcestershire sauce, Tabasco sauce, pepper, lemon juice, and celery salt to a shaker containing ice, and roll it gently to mix the ingredients.

❷ Pour into a highball glass and garnish with a wedge of lemon and lime, and a tender celery stick.

. . . .

ADAPT This is a super tasty version of a Virgin Mary—it's almost a liquid lunch. I recommend transferring it to a thermos and taking it on a long morning walk in the fresh air to revive you halfway. If you do use a thermos, chill the Bloody Bull beforehand and don't use ice, as the drink will become too diluted.

Chile and Lime Margarita

Serves 1

You will need
large pitcher; tumbler

5 ounces (150 ml) freshly
squeezed lime juice

1½ ounces (50 ml)
Chile-Infused Syrup
(page 24)

1 ounce (25 ml) freshly
squeezed orange juice

3 limes, thinly sliced

Fine sea salt

Wedge of lime

Ice cubes

Slices of lime to garnish

❶ Combine the lime juice, chile syrup,
orange juice, and sliced limes in a pitcher
and allow to stand for 10 minutes.

❷ Pour some salt on to a plate, slide the
wedge of lime around the rim of the glass,
and then dip the glass in the salt.

❸ Fill the glass with the margarita and ice
and serve garnished with slices of lime.

INSPIRATION I first tasted chile and lime
margaritas with my family at a beach bar
in Noosa, Australia. It was after a long
flight, and I've been in love with them
ever since. This recipe is a take on that
fabulous drink and I think it hits the spot,
whether you're by the seaside or at home
on a Sunday morning.

Beet Virgin Mary

Serves 2

You will need

juicer; pitcher; 2 tall glasses

6 cups (800 g) smallish beets, scrubbed, topped, tailed, and roughly chopped, or 16 ounces (500 ml) store-bought beet juice

Juice of 2 limes (reserve the juiced halves)

1 teaspoon Tabasco sauce

1 teaspoon Worcestershire sauce

1 teaspoon celery salt

Sea salt and freshly ground black pepper

Ice cubes

Freshly grated horseradish to garnish (you can keep this ready-peeled in the freezer or can grate from frozen using a Microplane grater)

2 celery sticks to stir

1 Juice the beets, if not using store-bought juice, and set aside. It's worth noting that small beets tend to have a milder flavor.

2 Mix the lime juice, Tabasco and Worcestershire sauces, and the celery salt together in a pitcher, add the beet juice, and put it in the fridge to cool.

3 If you like, rub the juiced lime halves around the rims of the tall glasses, then dip the rims into a saucer containing the salt and freshly ground pepper. Otherwise, simply fill the glasses with ice and top up with the beet juice. Add some freshly grated horseradish and serve with a celery stick.

HEALTHY This is a healthier version of the classic Bloody Mary, using beet juice as the base, which is very easy to make yourself if you have a juicer. If your beet is organic, there's no need to peel it in advance. This nutrient-rich juice is earthy and sweet, but be mindful that beets have the highest sugar content of any vegetable.

Strawberry Booster

Serves 1

You will need
blender; small tumbler

1 heaping tablespoon raw honey

Juice of 1 large lemon

Pinch of sea salt

1½ ounces (50 ml) hot water

Small handful ripe strawberries, hulled (smaller berries tend to taste better)

6 mint leaves

Splash of good-quality balsamic vinegar

Ice cubes

Chilled water, still or sparkling

Sprig of mint to garnish

1 Put the honey, lemon juice, salt, and hot water in a blender. Blend carefully for a few seconds, then add the strawberries and pulse the mixture until it's lovely and frothy.

2 Add the mint leaves and a splash of balsamic vinegar before blending again for 5 seconds more.

3 Pour the drink over ice and top with chilled water, either still or sparkling, and garnish with a sprig of mint.

. . . .

FLAVOR This delicious strawberry drink is the perfect antidote to that morning-after feeling, or the ideal post-workout tonic. The addition of the salt, balsamic vinegar, and lemon makes the fruit taste richer and sweeter.

Paloma Fizz

Serves 1

You will need

tumbler

2 ounces (60 ml) pink
  grapefruit juice

Pinch of Himalayan salt
  or sea salt

2 tablespoons Simple
  Herb Syrup made with
  rosemary (page 22)

Crushed ice

5 ounces (150 ml)
  sparkling water or
  grapefruit soda

Sprig of rosemary to
  garnish

❶ Pour the grapefruit juice into the
tumbler and stir in the pinch of salt and
rosemary syrup.

❷ Fill the glass with ice and then top up
with sparkling water. Garnish with the
sprig of rosemary.

FLAVOR Grapefruit, high in vitamin C
and potassium, is a great way to start the
day, and pink grapefruit has the added
benefit of being rich in beta-carotene. This
is a pretty, colorful, and refreshing drink
with a hint of savory rosemary. It takes a
simple glass of morning grapefruit juice to
a brand-new level.

Watermelon Mary

Serves 4

You will need
blender; 4 tall glasses

Flesh of ½ small
watermelon, seeded
and chopped

2 pounds (1 kg) ripe
tomatoes, peeled, or 2
cups (500 ml) good-
quality tomato juice

1 red bell pepper, seeded

1 garlic clove, peeled and
chopped

Pinch of sea salt

2½ ounces (75 ml)
organic apple cider
vinegar

3½ ounces (100 ml) olive
oil

Ice cubes

Seeds of a passion fruit
to garnish

❶ Blend the watermelon, tomatoes, red
bell pepper, garlic, and salt together, then
add the vinegar and olive oil slowly.

❷ Half-fill each glass with ice and pour in
a serving of juice. Top with passion fruit
seeds. If making a pitcher, chill in the
fridge for several hours before serving.

. . . .

INSPIRATION I was first given a bowl of
refreshing watermelon gazpacho on a hot
sunny day in Portugal. It was made from
a recipe from a Colombian friend and it
completely surpassed the straightforward
tomato version I was used to. This version
is a great what's-the-secret-ingredient
drink—people rarely guess watermelon!

Iced Cardamom Coffee

Serves 2

You will need

*coffee grinder or
powerful blender; mortar
and pestle; canning jar
or large lidded container;
fine-mesh sieve;
cheesecloth; 2 tumblers*

¾ cup (100 g) coarse-
grind roasted coffee,
or 8 tablespoons ready
ground coffee

8 green cardamom pods

1 quart (1 L) cold water
(the ratio of coffee to
water should be 1:8, so
increase the quantities
accordingly to make
more)

Ice cubes

Milk, cream, whipped
cream, and/or sugar
syrup

❶ If freshly grinding the coffee beans,
set the grinder to its most coarse setting.
You're looking for coffee grounds the same
consistency as breadcrumbs. If you don't
have a grinder, use a powerful blender.

❷ Pound the cardamom pods in a mortar
with a pestle, then discard the skin of the
pods before crushing the seeds lightly.

❸ Sterilize a large canning jar or any
large container with a lid and place the
cardamom and ground coffee in the jar.
Cover with the cold water, stir well, close
the lid, and leave the mixture for 18 to 24
hours, either in or out of the fridge.

❹ Strain the mixture through a fine-mesh
sieve over a large bowl, then repeat two
or three times through a clean piece of
cheesecloth or a few sheets of paper towel
until the coffee is clear. If it stays a bit murky,
it simply means your grind was too fine.

❺ Pour over ice and, if you like, add cold
milk, cream, or whipped cream. With or
without a touch of sugar syrup, this is a
wonderfully refreshing drink for a warm day.

....

ADAPT Cinnamon, hazelnut, and vanilla
are equally delicious in iced coffee, or
you could add the Spice Syrup on page 24
instead of the sugar syrup.

Raw Rhubarb Spritz

Serves 1

You will need
tall glass

Ice cubes

3 ounces (80 ml)
  Sweetened Raw
  Rhubarb Juice
  (recipe below)

Juice of ½ lime

Sparkling water

Trimmed rhubarb stick
  to stir

❶ Fill the glass with several pieces of ice and pour in the rhubarb juice.

❷ Add the lime juice and top with sparkling water. Use a stick of rhubarb to stir.

. . . .

FLAVOR When the first pink stalks of rhubarb start to push up through the winter earth, I really feel spring is just around the corner. This spritz tastes and smells intensely of rhubarb, undiluted by any cooking. Raw rhubarb—but on no account the leaf, which is poisonous—is delicious dipped in either sugar or salt.

Sweetened Raw Rhubarb Juice

You will need
blender; fine-mesh sieve

About 20 stalks (1 kg)
  rhubarb, trimmed of
  leaves and cut into
  ½-inch (1 cm) pieces

¾ cup (150 g) superfine
  sugar

❶ In a large bowl toss the rhubarb with the sugar and cover with plastic wrap. Leave in the fridge for at least 6 hours or, ideally, overnight.

❷ Place the rhubarb into a blender along with all the juice that has collected in the bowl, and blitz for 1 minute. Push the mixture through a fine-mesh sieve, collecting the liquid in a bowl beneath.

❸ Pour into a sterilized bottle. It will keep in the fridge for a few days.

LONG SUMMERS

The high sun, long evenings, and heady scents of summer are an invitation to laze around outside, sipping cool drinks with friends. Fruits are ripe, bees hum in the lavender, and a sweet-scented garden or park provides the perfect excuse to turn a quick drink into an impromptu gathering. All of these drinks are fragrant, cool, and can be transformed easily from a single glass into a sociable pitcher.

Black Currant Shrub Summer Cup

Serves 1

You will need

muddler; highball

Handful mint or lemon
   verbena leaves

Ice cubes

1¼ ounces (40 ml)
   Black Currant Shrub
   (page 23)

1 teaspoon rose water

5 ounces (150 ml)
   sparkling water

Curl of lemon peel, plus
   mint leaves and a sprig
   of black currants to
   garnish

❶ Lightly bruise the mint or lemon
verbena leaves by placing them in a glass
and squashing them with the muddler.

❷ Half-fill the glass with ice, then pour
in the shrub and add about a teaspoon of
rose water, to taste. You're aiming for a
light scent of summer roses, so go gently
and add more, drop by drop, if needed.

❸ Top up with sparkling water. Garnish
the glass with some mint leaves, a curl of a
lemon peel, and a sprig of black currants.

....

INSPIRATION This drink reminds me of
long summer days in England as a child,
guzzling icy Ribena. I remember being
called over, gulping down the sweet tang
of black currant, then rushing back out to
play. This is a more grown-up version.

Passion Fruit and Lime Sparkler

Serves 1

You will need

muddler; tumbler

½ lime, cut into wedges

Good handful of mint leaves

1 tablespoon superfine sugar

2 slices of fresh ginger, peeled

2 passion fruit, cut in half (reserve one half to garnish)

Ice cubes

Sparkling water

Wedge of lime to garnish

❶ Muddle the lime wedges, mint leaves, and sugar together in a glass. Add the ginger and the juice and seeds of three halves of passion fruit.

❷ Fill the glass with ice, add sparkling water, and stir. Garnish with passion fruit seeds and a wedge of lime.

. . . .

INSPIRATION Passion fruit is incredibly zesty and full of flavor. It always makes me think of hot countries and tropical days. So this passion fruit and lime sparkler was designed with summer in mind, and is a great way to cool down after a day in the sun.

Drivers' Pimm's Cup

Serves 4

You will need

small pitcher; larger pitcher; 4 highballs

1½ ounces (40 ml) brewed black tea

½ teaspoon dark brown sugar

1½ ounces (40 ml) ginger beer or 2 teaspoons (10 ml) Ginger and Black Peppercorn Syrup (page 23) and 1 ounce (30 ml) soda water

½ teaspoon good-quality balsamic vinegar

Ice cubes

2 oranges, sliced

2 lemons, sliced

Slices of cucumber

Lemonade

Borage flowers and sprigs of mint to garnish

❶ Make a cup of strong black tea. Pour 1½ ounces (40 ml) of the tea into a small pitcher, then stir in the sugar and leave to cool. Once cool, add the ginger beer and balsamic vinegar.

❷ Fill a serving pitcher or some chilled tall glasses with ice cubes and the sliced fruits and cucumber.

❸ Add one part Drivers' Pimm's to three parts lemonade. Decorate with borage flowers and sprigs of mint.

. . . .

INSPIRATION Pimm's was one of the first drinks I was ever given in my grandparents' garden, and it always reminds me of long, easy family lunches that drift lazily into the evening.

Cucumber and Elderflower Cooler

Serves 1

You will need
muddler; highball

Handful of fresh basil

4 slices of cucumber

1 lime, cut into wedges

1½ ounces (40 ml)
  elderflower cordial

¾ ounce (20 ml) Simple
  Herb Syrup made with
  rosemary (page 22)

A dash of freshly
  squeezed lime juice

Crushed ice

Sparkling water

A sprig of basil,
  cucumber slices, and
  long baton of cucumber
  to garnish

❶ Muddle the basil, cucumber, and lime wedges in a highball. Add the elderflower cordial, rosemary syrup, and dash of lime juice.

❷ Half-fill the glass with crushed ice, then top up with sparkling water.

❸ Stir everything together and garnish with a sprig of basil, cucumber slices, and a long baton of cucumber.

....

FLAVOR This is a deliciously sophisticated drink with aromatic back notes of basil and rosemary. The cucumber gives the drink a clean, green freshness, which makes it the perfect aperitif.

ADAPT It's also wonderful made with fresh mint instead of basil.

Ginger Fever

Serves 4

You will need

muddler; large pitcher; 4 tumblers

½ stalk lemongrass, thinly sliced

½ cup (120 ml) Ginger and Black Peppercorn Syrup (page 23)

Juice of 2 limes

Ice cubes

3 cups (750 ml) ginger beer

4 strips of orange peel and 4 wedges of lime to garnish

Stalk of lemongrass sliced lengthwise to use as swizzle stick

1 Lightly bash the lemongrass with a muddler and place it in a large pitcher.

2 Pour in the ginger syrup and the lime juice, then Half-fill the pitcher with ice. Top it up with ginger beer.

3 Divide the contents of the pitcher between the 4 glasses. Twist a strip of orange peel over each glass to release the oils before dropping it in. Serve each with a wedge of lime and a lemongrass swizzle stick.

. . . .

INSPIRATION When he arrived home from work, my father would always pour himself a gin and ginger beer. With the aromatic, bright citrus notes of lemongrass cutting through the warmth of the ginger, this simple, restorative drink signals the end of the day to me.

Still Rose Lemonade

Serves 4

You will need

heatproof bowl; large pitcher; 4 tumblers

4 large lemons, sliced

Heaping ⅓ cup (80 g) sugar

2 cups (500 ml) boiling water

1 to 2 teaspoons rose water (to taste), or a dash of Simple Flower Syrup made with rose-scented geranium leaves (page 22)

Ice cubes

❶ Put the lemons and sugar into a heatproof bowl and cover them with the boiling water.

❷ Stir until the sugar has dissolved. Allow the liquid to cool, then mix in the rose water or rose-geranium syrup a little at a time, tasting as you go. It should be very lemony with just a hint of rose.

❸ Fill a pitcher with ice and pour in the lemonade ready to serve.

. . . .

SERVING SUGGESTION The essence of summer. Refreshing zesty lemons with a hint of fragrant rose. This is a fabulous drink to take on a picnic. Before you set off, fill a large thermos or sealable pitcher with ice and pour in the lemonade. By the time you arrive, the ice will have melted, leaving a deliciously cool, thirst-quenching treat.

Summer Storm

Serves 1

You will need

blender; shaker; coupe; strainer

½ cup (100 g) ripe pineapple, peeled, cored and cut into chunks

1 ounce (25 ml) Ginger and Black Peppercorn Syrup (page 23)

½ ounce (15 ml) organic egg white

Ice cubes

1 small piece of preserved ginger

Sparkling water

① Blend the pineapple for about 30 seconds until it's crushed but not puréed.

② Mix 3½ ounces (100 ml) of the pineapple with the ginger syrup and the egg white in a cocktail shaker. Add the ice cubes and shake again.

③ Put the ginger in the glass and strain in the cocktail. Top it up with a little sparkling water.

....

FLAVOR The peppery ginger syrup cuts through the sweetness and enhances the tart, fragrant qualities of the pineapple. Just imagine sipping this sitting on a veranda, while warm tropical rain thunders on the roof.

Roasted Peach Lemonade

Serves 2

You will need
*baking dish; blender;
pitcher; 2 coupes*

4 medium peaches, sliced
  in half and pitted

1 tablespoon sugar

2 cups (500 ml)
  homemade lemonade
  (follow the recipe for
  Still Rose Lemonade on
  page 96 but omit the
  rose water)

Ice cubes

Sparkling water

❶ Preheat the oven to 390°F (200°C) /
360°F (180°C) convection.

❷ Place the peaches skin side down in
a baking dish and sprinkle with sugar.
Roast for about 25 minutes, until the tops
are juicy and the skins are easy to pinch
off.

❸ Put the roasted, skinned peaches in
a blender and add enough lemonade to
cover them. Blitz until the peaches are
puréed completely and the liquid is a little
foamy and frothy.

❹ Pour the mixture into a pitcher and stir
in the rest of the lemonade. Allow to cool.
Before serving, add the ice and top up with
a bit of sparkling water.

. . . .

FLAVOR A perfectly ripe peach evokes
the scents of honey, rose, and summer,
and roasting the fruit produces a warm
caramel flavor to enhance this summery
drink.

WOOD SMOKE WARMERS

*As autumn begins, the light softens,
fires are lit, and we bundle up to
go apple and pumpkin picking.
Fragrant apples are ready to pick,
and I find myself pausing while
wandering to sip a delicious, spiced
drink from a thermos. Make the
drinks in this chapter to have by a
bonfire or for when you arrive home
with cold-flushed cheeks and
chilly hands.*

Autumn Sangria

Serves 2

You will need:
large pitcher, 2 large goblets

1 apple, thinly sliced (using a mandoline if possible)

½ small pear, thinly sliced (using a mandoline if possible)

1 red plum, sliced into wedges

½ small orange, sliced

Handful of pitted cherries, fresh or frozen

5 ounces (150 ml) apple juice, chilled

2½ ounces (75 ml) freshly squeezed orange juice

1 teaspoon Ginger and Black Peppercorn Syrup (see page 23)

Ice cubes

Tonic water

2 sprigs of mint to garnish

❶ In a pitcher, combine all the fruit with the apple juice, orange juice, and ginger syrup, then refrigerate for a couple of hours.

❷ Once chilled, divide between 2 large goblets filled with ice, top up with tonic water, and garnish with a sprig of mint.

FLAVOR This recipe is just a guideline. It's a generous, bountiful drink and I particularly enjoy using a mixture of different apples to make it. If you have an apple tree in your garden, or access to one, use fresh apple juice. You could also juice apples from the supermarket. When the quantities are scaled up, this looks wonderful in a large pitcher, so throw in the fruits you gather and share it with friends.

Warming Dark Berry Shrub

Serves 1

You will need:
heatproof glass

5 ounces (150 ml) apple
   juice

Slice of lemon

2 bay leaves

1½ ounces (50 ml) Berry
   Shrub made with
   blackberries (see page
   23)

1 tablespoon honey

Bay leaf to garnish,
   preferably fresh

❶ Gently warm the apple juice in a pan
with the lemon slice and the 2 bay leaves.
Simmer over a low heat for 5 minutes to
allow the flavors to infuse. Do not let it
boil.

❷ Add the blackberry shrub and honey,
and stir until dissolved.

❸ Make sure the drink is warm enough,
then pour the liquid into a heatproof glass
and garnish with a bay leaf.

....

FLAVOR For me, the pairing of tart deep-
purple blackberries and sweet aromatic
apple signals autumn. The wonderful color
and scented steam of this drink certainly
keep the chilly wind at bay.

Cranberry and Hibiscus Allspice

Serves 1

You will need:
strainer; heatproof glass,

1 cup (250 ml) cranberry juice

3 allspice berries

1 cinnamon stick

Slice of fresh ginger, peeled

1 star anise

½ teaspoon Sichuan peppercorns or black peppercorns

1 bay leaf

Pinch of dried hibiscus petals or a flower

1 ounce (25 ml) Hibiscus Syrup (page 24)

1 Add all the ingredients except the hibiscus syrup to a pan, then cover and simmer over a low heat for about 10 minutes.

2 Add the hibiscus syrup and taste. You're looking for a balance between sweet and tart, with just a hint of spice.

3 Strain the liquid to remove the whole spices and bay leaf but put the hibiscus flower, cinnamon stick, and ginger slice back into the strained liquid.

4 Serve straight away in a heatproof glass or pour into a thermos for later.

FLAVOR The fragrant steam showcases the very best of autumn and winter spices, while the hibiscus gives an unusual and sharp lemony note.

ADAPT A welcoming warm, ruby-colored, spiced drink to banish the darkening nights, this is particularly delicious when served with spiced cookies for dunking. Crisp biscotti work especially well.

Hot Buttered Spiced Apple

Serves 1

You will need:
heatproof glass or mug

1 cup (250 ml) unfiltered
    apple juice

Juice of ½ lemon, plus
    1 strip of zest

Juice of ½ orange, plus
    1 strip of zest

½ cinnamon stick

1 whole clove

2 allspice berries

¼ teaspoon fennel seeds

Small red chile (optional)

½ teaspoon unsalted
    butter, softened

Cinnamon stick for
    garnish

❶ Add the apple juice, lemon juice, orange juice, zests, spices, and fennel seeds to a pan. Simmer over a medium heat for 20 minutes but do not allow to boil.

❷ If you're adding chile, do so halfway through and keep tasting. Remove if it starts to become too spicy. The idea is to add a little gentle background heat that is barely noticeable.

❸ Ladle the liquid into a heatproof glass or mug, leaving the zest and spices in the pan if you wish.

❹ Add about half a teaspoon of butter to the glass. Serve with a cinnamon stick to garnish.

....

INSPIRATION I've had many versions of hot apple juice or cider over the years, but this is one of my favorites. It's incredibly warming at the end of a long walk or on arriving home after a cold, busy day.

FLAVOR It might sound odd to use butter in a drink, but it adds a lovely savory depth. You can also play with the flavors a little—add citrus zest or a pinch of ground cinnamon to your softened butter, or add a dash of maple syrup if your apples are a little tart.

Thai Coconut Tea

Serves 2

You will need:
2 tall heatproof glasses

2 cups (500 ml) water

2 black tea bags

¼ cup (45 g) sugar

2 star anise

1 green cardamom pod, smashed

2 whole cloves

½ vanilla pod, split in half, or ¼ teaspoon vanilla extract

3 tablespoons (90 ml) coconut milk

2 lemongrass stalks to stir

❶ Bring a pan containing 2 cups (500 ml) water to boil and add the tea bags, sugar, star anise, cardamom pod, and whole cloves. Stir the ingredients together until all of the sugar has dissolved.

❷ Boil for 3 minutes more, then remove from the heat and add the vanilla pod or extract. Allow the tea to steep for at least 30 minutes, preferably an hour.

❸ Remove the tea bags and spices and discard. Reheat the liquid gently, then divide between 2 heatproof glasses.

❹ Spoon the coconut milk on top—if the milk is very thick, whisk in a little normal milk or coconut water until it's easy to pour. Add a stalk of lemongrass to each glass to stir.

ADAPT This will keep happily in the fridge for a few days without the coconut milk, so it might be worth making a larger volume and saving some for later. It also tastes fantastic chilled. Just fill the glasses with ice, pour in the cold tea and float the coconut milk on top.

Smoke and Ruby Tumbler

Serves 1

You will need:
tumbler

4 ounces (120 ml)
freshly squeezed ruby
grapefruit juice

Ice cubes

¾ ounce (20 ml)
Smoky Lapsang Syrup
(page 23)

Good squeeze of lemon
juice

Strip of grapefruit peel to
garnish

❶ Pour the grapefruit juice over ice in a small tumbler and then add the syrup to taste. You're aiming for a sweet, smoky background to the brighter, citrusy grapefruit.

❷ Add a good squeeze of lemon juice and stir. Garnish with a strip of grapefruit peel.

....

FLAVOR Lapsang syrup provides a hint of the smoky, caramel taste of a Highland single malt whiskey. When partnered with tart grapefruit, it's delicious to drink by a bonfire when your cheeks are hot and your feet are cold.

Pear and Rosemary on the Rocks

Serves 1

You will need:
shaker; strainer; tumbler

2 ounces (60 ml) pear
juice from 2 small
pears, or good-quality
store-bought pear juice
(not from concentrate)

1 ounce (30 ml) freshly
squeezed lemon juice

1 ounce (25 ml) Simple
Herb Syrup made with
rosemary (page 22)

Ice cubes

Sparkling water

Sprig of rosemary and a
slice of pear to garnish

Lemonade (optional)

❶ Combine the pear juice, lemon juice,
and rosemary syrup in a cocktail shaker
with ice, and shake well.

❷ Strain into a tumbler and top with a
splash of sparkling water. Garnish with a
sprig of rosemary and a slice of pear. For a
longer drink, add more water and a dash of
lemonade.

....

FLAVOR This is an elegant drink for an
autumn evening, as the shadows begin to
lengthen and a chill appears in the air. For
me, a ripe pear is a luscious and fragrant
treat, particularly when paired with a hint
of warm, woody rosemary.

Earl Grey Hot Toddy

Serves 1

You will need:
heatproof glass or mug

1 Earl Grey tea bag

Sprig of thyme

1 cup (235 ml) boiling
water

2 tablespoons (30 ml)
freshly squeezed
lemon juice

Honey

Thin slice of lemon to
garnish

❶ Place the tea bag and thyme in a heatproof glass or mug. Cover them with boiling water and steep for 4 minutes.

❷ Remove the tea bag without pressing on it, then add the lemon juice. Stir gently and add honey to taste. Garnish with a thin slice of lemon.

FLAVOR A hot toddy is a must for chilly days. Earl Grey brings with it a hint of bergamot, which, when paired with aromatic lemon thyme, makes everything feel fresh and bright. This is perfect for thawing frozen fingers.

FIRESIDE GLOW

As the cold weather begins to creep in, a crackling fire and drinks to sip with family and friends are essential. When you're snuggled up at home, these drinks will warm your taste buds and your spirit.

Blackberry Seedlip Smash

Serves 1

You will need:
muddler; tumbler

5 large blackberries

½ lime

1 tablespoon sugar

Crushed ice

1 ounce (30 ml) Seedlip
  Spice 94

Sparkling water

Slice of lime to garnish

❶ Muddle the blackberries with the lime and sugar in a tumbler.

❷ Partially fill the glass with crushed ice, add the Seedlip, and top up with sparkling water. Serve with a slice of lime.

INSPIRATION The thrill of heading home from blackberry-picking with a bag full of dark juicy fruit never disappears. Jake, my dog, stands resignedly as I promise, "Just that last bush, then we'll go home." Your fingers may be scratched and stained but the bounty is worth it.

After Eight Martini

Serves 1

You will need:

strainer; shaker; chilled martini glass

1 tablespoon Chocolate Ganache (recipe below)

1½ ounces (50 ml) heavy cream

1 ounce (30 ml) Simple Herb Syrup made with mint (page 22)

Ice cubes

Mint leaf or sprig to garnish

① Put a tablespoon of ganache into a pan with the cream and mint syrup, and heat very gently until the ingredients are blended.

② Allow the mixture to cool, then pour into a shaker with some cubes of ice, and shake.

③ Working quickly, strain the drink into a chilled martini glass and garnish with a leaf or sprig of mint.

INSPIRATION This is a real after-dinner treat, rich and chocolaty with a hint of mint. I remember stealing After Eight chocolates from my grandparents as a child, and feeling deliciously wicked while licking sticky fingers.

Chocolate Ganache

1 cup (235 ml) heavy cream

9 ounces (250 g) good-quality dark chocolate, grated

① Put the cream in a pan and heat gently. Bring just to the point of boiling and keep watch to stop it from boiling over. Add the grated chocolate and whisk until smooth.

② Transfer to a sterilized container and store in the fridge. It will keep happily for up to a month, but keep it well covered so it doesn't absorb any fridge flavors. It doesn't take long to make and is also delicious whisked into a cup of hot milk on a cold, gray afternoon.

Fragrant Tea Flower Punch

Serves 2

You will need:

heatproof bowl; pitcher or jar; 2 heatproof glasses

3½ ounces (100 ml) freshly squeezed lemon juice

1 cup (250 ml) clear or unfiltered apple juice

1 flowering jasmine tea bud

2½ cups (600 ml) boiling water

3½ ounces (100 ml) Spice Syrup (page 24)

2 thin slices of lemon to garnish

❶ Put the lemon juice and apple juice in a pan. Warm gently but don't allow to boil.

❷ Place the tea bud in a heatproof bowl and add the boiling water.

❸ After a few minutes, once the tea bud has unfurled, add the spice syrup and warmed fruit juices. Taste and add more syrup or lemon juice, if needed.

❹ Serve in heatproof glasses with a thin slice of lemon to garnish.

. . . .

FLAVOR This is a light and fruity yet warm and spicy punch with the wonderful scent of a tea flower. And there's something very exotic about bringing a fragrant bowl of punch to share between friends.

Vanilla Cranberry Cocktail

Serves 1

You will need:

shaker; chilled coupe or martini glass

½ teaspoon finely grated orange zest

½ teaspoon finely grated lime zest

½ tablespoon (10 ml) freshly squeezed lime juice

3½ ounces (100 ml) cranberry juice

1 scoop good-quality vanilla ice cream

3 to 5 fresh or frozen cranberries or raspberries to garnish

❶ Combine the orange and lime zests, lime juice, cranberry juice, and vanilla ice cream in a shaker, and shake vigorously.

❷ Pour into a chilled glass and allow to stand for a few seconds so that the foam settles. Decorate with fresh or frozen cranberries or raspberries.

FLAVOR A fireside treat, this cocktail reminds me of winter sunsets. It's a fruity, creamy, not-too-sweet pudding in a glass.

Espresso Mint Martini

Serves 1

You will need:

strainer; shaker; chilled martini glass

3½ ounces (100 ml) brewed espresso

Ice cubes

1 ounce (25 ml) Simple Herb Syrup made with mint (page 22)

① Make a strong espresso and allow to cool before pouring over ice cubes in a shaker.

② Working quickly, add the mint syrup and shake vigorously. The faster your shaking, the greater the chance of getting a lovely espresso head of foam. Strain into a chilled martini glass.

. . . .

ADAPT There's something very grown-up about an espresso martini, and this is a great after-dinner fireside drink, with just a hint of mint. I sometimes like to add a few drops of almond extract and a splash of sugar syrup in place of the mint syrup. If it's late at night, this martini is just as delicious made with decaf espresso.

Mexican Chile Cacao

Serves 1

You will need:
heatproof bowl and glass

1 cinnamon stick

½ ancho chile

5 ounces (150 ml) milk of your choice

2 ounces (50 g) good-quality dark chocolate, chopped or finely grated

1 teaspoon light muscovado sugar

Pinch of sea salt

Dark chocolate shavings to garnish

Cinnamon stick to stir

❶ Add the cinnamon stick and the ancho chile to the milk and simmer over a low heat until fragrant, which will probably take 5 to 10 minutes.

❷ Add the chopped chocolate to a heatproof bowl. Remove the cinnamon stick and the ancho chile from the hot milk, add the sugar and a pinch of salt, and pour the milk over the chocolate.

❸ Whisk them together until they're thick and frothy. Serve immediately in a heatproof glass, garnished with chocolate shavings and a cinnamon stick.

FLAVOR This is a real treat for when you're in need of a bit of nurturing. The ancho chile adds a depth of flavor and mild, sweet heat to the warm chocolate. It's perfect for snuggling up with under a blanket on a chilly afternoon, or for sipping by a roaring bonfire.

Tamarind Spice Glow

Serves 1

You will need:

heatproof glass or cup

1 teaspoon pure tamarind paste

1 teaspoon Spice Syrup (page 24)

1¼ cup (300 ml) not quite boiling water

2 thin slices of lemon

Crushed ice (optional)

1 Add the tamarind paste and spice syrup to a heatproof glass or cup and mix together with a little of the hot water.

2 Top up with the rest of the water and add a slice or two of lemon. If you want to serve it chilled, pour the cooled liquid over a glass of crushed ice before you add the lemon slice.

....

FLAVOR Tamarind paste comes from the fruit pods of tamarind trees found in Asia, and has a delicious sweet-tart taste. It's unique and hints at exotic places, marrying well with lightly spiced syrup to soften the sourness, and is full of antioxidants. The pods need to be soaked in water for about 15 minutes, then mashed and strained to extract the seeds and paste. The paste can be found prepared in supermarkets but make sure it's pure tamarind and not a sauce.

Pomegranate Negroni

Serves 1

You will need:
tumbler

7 ounces (200 ml) pure
   pomegranate juice

2 teaspoons
   Montmorency cherry
   concentrate

Ice cubes

3 good dashes of
   Angostura bitters

Twist of orange peel

Pour the pomegranate juice and cherry concentrate into a glass of ice, then stir well before shaking in the Angostura bitters. The drink should have a bitter-sweet tang, so add more Angostura if needed. Twist the orange peel on top of the drink to release the oils.

FLAVOR The cherry concentrate gives an extra layer, but isn't essential. However, I recommend keeping the cherry concentrate in the fridge as a sugar-free cordial. It's also delicious with hot water.